Nose

Julie Murray

Peachtree

Abdo
YOUR BODY
Kids

abdopublishing.com

Published by Abdo Kids, a division of ABDO, PO Box 398166, Minneapolis, Minnesota 55439.
Copyright © 2016 by Abdo Consulting Group, Inc. International copyrights reserved in all countries.
No part of this book may be reproduced in any form without written permission from the publisher.

Printed in the United States of America, North Mankato, Minnesota.

102015

012016

 THIS BOOK CONTAINS
RECYCLED MATERIALS

Photo Credits: iStock, Shutterstock

Production Contributors: Teddy Borth, Jennie Forsberg, Grace Hansen

Design Contributors: Candice Keimig, Dorothy Toth

Library of Congress Control Number: 2015941972

Cataloging-in-Publication Data

Murray, Julie.

 Nose / Julie Murray.

   p. cm. -- (Your body)

ISBN 978-1-68080-161-3 (lib. bdg.)

Includes index.

1. Nose--Juvenile literature. 2. Smell--Juvenile literature.   I. Title.

612.8/6--dc23

                    2015941972

Table of Contents

Nose

The nose is a part of your body.

Sue touches her nose.

5

Your nose has two holes.

These are called **nostrils**.

Your nose lets you smell.

Dan smells flowers.

You can smell good smells.

John smells cookies.

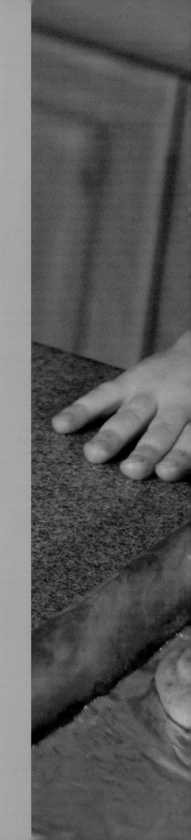

You can smell bad smells.

Ryan smells trash.

Your nose can be **stuffy**.

Mary has a cold.

You breathe through your nose.

Kate takes a breath.

Animals have noses too.

Pigs have a good sense of smell!

What do you like to smell?

Parts of the Nose

Dorsum

Ala

Apex

Nostril

Columella

Glossary

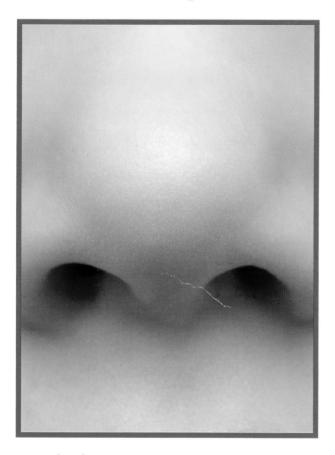

nostrils
two holes that allow you to breathe through your nose.

stuffy
a way to describe your nose if it is hard to breathe due illness or allergies.

Index

abdokids.com

Use this code to log on to abdokids.com and access crafts, games, videos, and more!

Abdo Kids Code:
YNK1613